Anima/l

Fiona Owen

Published by Cinnamon Press
www.cinnamonpress.com

ISBN 978-1-78864-163-0

British Library Cataloguing in Publication Data. A CIP record for this book can be obtained from the British Library.

Designed and typeset in Bodini by Cinnamon Press. Cover design by Adam Craig © Adam Craig from original artwork, 'Hare, collage' by Ann Johnson © Ann Johnson, used with kind permission, from the series 'Creatura' (https://creatura2016.wordpress.com/)

Cinnamon Press is represented by Inpress.

Acknowledgements

Heartfelt thanks to Ann Johnson for use of her 'Hare, collage' for the cover image, and to Seán Street, Menna Elfyn and Paul Matthews for taking the time to read the collection and write some words about it. Diolch o galon. Thanks also to Seán for the book's epigraph quotation.

Special thanks to Jan & Adam of Cinnamon Press for their on-going support and patience.

Various poems in this collection have been published in the following magazines, journals and anthologies, with thanks due to the editors: *Red Poets; Raceme; Black Bough Poetry; The Kith Review; Scintilla; A Bee's Breakfast; Coed; From Hallows to Harvest; Noble Dissent; Onward/Ymlaen; Well, Dam; Poetry for Ukraine: Poetry in support of Ukraine, from Poets around the World.*

'The Way a Cat Interrupts' won first prize, many moons ago, in a Cotswold writer's competition.

to celebrate the sanctity

of the everyday

Contents

Hildegard's Birds	9
A Year's Turning	13
Conservatory	18
Anima/l	20
Rōshi	26
That Cat in Three Movements	28
Two Summer Rain Songs	31
Lead-up to Lockdown	32
The Old Places	36
Susie's Card	38
Blue Beltane	39
Summer's Lease	40
Lammas	41
Last of Summer	42
Autumn Equinox	43
September's Bird	44
The Dark Time	45
On Observing the Mulberry in November	46
The Start of Fox's Dissent	47
On hearing of Jo Cox's last words	48
Morning After	49
Home Haibun 2021	50
From Lost Sequence with John	55
Mental Fly	56
Ambulant	57
Veg Patch	58
The Teaching of Trees	60
Aberffraw	61
Sŵn cŵn / Dogs bark	62
Noson Hydref / Autumn Evening	63
Crab-Apple Sequence	64
Three Summer Haibun	68
Ting	70
Key	71
Abel's Angel	72
Deer Heart	73

Rowing   74
How You Won Her   75
Pugilist 1   76
Pugilist 2   77
Lament   78
Rosebuds in Blue   79
Too Lonely   80
Soul's Bird   81
Aunty Toss Comes for a Visit   82
At a Victorian Victualler's c.1890   83
First Mother   84
I'll Give You Chick   85
Going to Hell   86
Selfies for Peace   87
Nana's Cabinet   88
If Only   90
Ready, Lads?   91
Moment   92
Anniversary of Dad's Death   93
Viriditas   94
Threshold   96
Friar Francis   98
Thank You, Heart   99
Notes on the poems   100

For Gorwel, always.

Fy Nghariad.

Also, my precious friends

& the many non-human animals

who have extended my circle of love so dearly.

Hildegard's Birds

The Word is living, being, spirit, all verdant greening, all creativity.
This Word manifests itself in every creature.

Hildegard Von Bingen

I opened my hands
and a myriad birds flew

from my warm palms
upturned

into the wide-open
blue

and when one bird entered,
I let it sing

carried on spirals
in my heart's blood
stream;

the birds flew high
in a spiral of light:

never let die the things
that bring you life.

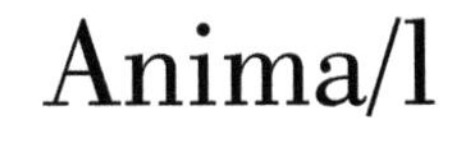

Anima/l

A Year's Turning

The time-being has the quality of flowing ...
                                        Dōgen

New Year's Day

It's a rook that watches,
at dusk, from its ink-etched
branch,
          a living sumi-e painting.

It draws night
into itself.

Sometimes

          we must endure
the days of drizzle,
                    the endless days
of low, where cloud has descended
and a fine rain wets to the bone.

People moan, but where would our *green* be
without cloud and rain?

Lao Tzu says *go with*—yet I've seen a grown man
fall to his knees and curse the sky with a raised fist
for rain's disobedience.

We can complain if we want to, but the weather
will do as it does.

Underground

There's preparatory fire
zinging in the blood
of this hearthy
moment.

Snowdrops are up
and it won't be long
before wood splits,
poeming the miraculous
into bright new green.

Stirring my coffee:
the small near *clink*
of spoon against the china
of my favourite cup.

Vernal Equinox

The dog in deep sleep beside me,
her dream-twitches and breath;

the sparrow by the bay tree
pecking at the slatey soil;

the breeze, always the breeze,
through the open window, damp
this morning after a warm spell

and it comes, like fragments of this
and that, lifting to relief the *bric-à-brac*—

this small sacrament of naming,
as the year, the moment, tilts towards
its next becoming—

Mulberry

        keeps
ts leafage
        till late
so it's still bare at Beltane.

Everything else is putting on leaf,
budding and buddying, relief
after long winter blasts
stopped the sap.

I, too, am sensing the time
to shed winter

and go for hearts.

See how quickly

months come & go. Today,
rain.
            The wind wakes me
through the open window
too early.

            I lie contemplating
the unscheduled day:

can we ever know
what's in store?

Later, through the window,
fuchsia and lavender sprawl
together wantonly, while
something in me wants
to go wild.

The ferns

            have taken back
the veg patch we paid a man to clear
with his neat little digger that clawed
at the docks, lifted rocks, dragged at ivy
till the patch was back to barefaced soil

but look at it now: the dog rose, plush
along the fence where mullein and evening
primroses tower over the mayhem—and ivy's
back, with its lessons in tenacity, in cut, cut
and keep on coming again.

Late Summer

Wasps are at the apples,
gorging on the sugars
gathered in the flesh

culmination of the cycle

fruit setting in spring
despite wind that scattered
the pear tree's blossoms.
Into this late-summer apple, its red-
wash sheen,
                    a wasp bores deep,
its ardent body buried as it feasts

parable of the kin-dom, where wasps,
too, deserve their sweets.

Danse Macabre

Against the window
a miniature tapping—
it is a wasp
dead since Sunday.

A single strand
of spider-web
binds its leg
to the window frame.

In gusts of wind
come tiny raps
against the pane

as fierce life, turned
to husk,

softens in rain.

Blackberry

   drops
easy-does-it
     into
the hand.

It's ripeness
           that brings
yielding.

Life's art & craft
is to grow
            a feel
for timing.

There it sits,
this berry, perfect
in my palm,

its dark juice running
all along my lifeline.

I never tire

              of these trees
in their seasons—fallen
sepia leaves, loyal

to the seasonal round.

There's no saying what the year,
month, week, day or hour will bring,
what ground will be opened.

Conservatory

I come to fill in a boring form
but the sun is a fireball setting
between trees
                      and a skein of twelve
geese fly overhead, slow enough to count,
honking their passing
in that rasping way

so I set down my pen
till the last traces of them
have flown south, while

westwards flames
                          its spectacle
of cranberry colour
that spills all along the shoreline.

November

Litter of spent foliage
at the base of the tree, while
a few last leaves hang, yellowing,
on the brink of letting go.

A crow pecks at what's left
of the bread I put out, & blackbirds
feast on the Bramley windfalls.

It will be grey all day.

Your Birthday

Even as the year dwindles, and the grey of winter
lowers the skies, we drive out on your birthday
to the headland, where there's blurring cloud
and white-tipped choppy wide-open sea.

The lighthouse, on its promontory, flashes its light
into that wild expanse, saver of sailors' souls.

Culmination

Above
        the blaze—
and the bare birch

the sun, like an orange
lozenge,
        fizzes
into the Irish Sea.

Anima/1

After Flóra Borsi's self-portraits Animeyed

Thy Kin-dom come, thy Love be done
On earth as it is in heaven ...

I

I was amazed by the peculiarity of each species ...

I'm most like the one with the squirrel:
all that russet, light concentrate
points in each pupil, the squirrel snug
against my nose. I could be her,
a natural fit, with one animeye
to balance my human vision, the other
feeding dreams of bark and boles, acorns
gathered in winter dreys, with long summer
days among leaves, maxing out on green.

The whole word's mostly *soul*—'animal'
being 'any sentient living creature that breathes'.
Dependent on air, we are intimately adapted
to the alchemy of nitrogen, oxygen, argon,
water vapour, carbon dioxide and trace gases
that go over my head (and into my lungs—
I pause to notice my body background-breathing itself
as, outside, early August rain tinkles along gutters).

'Animal' used rarely before 1600 when non-humans
were called 'beasts' and humans who were beastly
were damned as 'animals': you pig, you rat, you dirty
dog, you chick chick chicken, you snake in the grass.

II

… and the similarity between humans and animals.

I am least like the one with the snake—or *am* I? Her face
is mud-encrusted, forest-lichened, the creature curled
around her neck like a curse or a question, and isn't that
the red of ripe apple on her lips? Together, they brought
the whole house down, so the story goes, but she's
owning it, gazing out as a 'we', in solidarity with snake
kind, green-eyed human colour-vision to balance
the serpent's black and white sightedness.

Oh yes, we needed to know what was outside the garden—
so the snake slipped through a hole in the wall and found
the woman's ready ear. He told her and she told the man
and the governing patriarchs heard dissent in the whispers.
That's when *story* was truly born, and whose story would win?

III

I wanted to show that we are very similar to them.

I recognise that look, the startled hare
in the headlights, or is it a rabbit? Same
wide-eyed difference—in the face of threat,
do you fight, flee or freeze? The latter. Light's
splashed on the face, into the eyes, like water
from a puddle in a road as the car bears down.

Is it light that's there to greet us on impact?

The prey animal knows in its blood and bones
that life's precarious. The rabbit's big ears
are all the better to hear with, but sometimes,
fear's chemicals stop you in your tracks.

Once, we stopped the car at night to move
an injured rabbit off the road that runs straight
and fast through Aberffraw common. A car came
speeding towards us, its lights dazzling on full
yet the driver didn't see him and it was close
to being tragic. He leapt to the side in time,
the rabbit in his arms. We weren't sure
it would even make it. Rabbit carcasses litter
that road. They suffer like us. Noble Truth No. 1.

IV

I also wanted to show how unique and special they are …

That neck, for a start, long and lithe, and all that pink.
Their tawny eyes gaze outwards and she's dyed her hair
to match, painted her lips a gorgeous sludge, like
the tip of the bird's beak. To be born into such a flamboyance
is to be, unknowingly, the height of *chic*, the exotic *other*,
lotus flower of the bird world, perfection from rooting
in mud, clever beaks adapted to the upside-down
scooping motion of filter-feeding on algae and shrimp
that turn their plumage pink. Life's imagination!

V

Yes, fish, too. They flap their gills and tails,
their whole bodies, when swimming, or drowning
in air. She's dyed her hair goldfish red, backcombed it
to match the dorsal fin, the whole thing orange—
eyebrows, lips—and pale, kin-coloured eyes meet our own.

Memory from childhood: Dad stops the car, gets out,
buys a big, just-caught fish from a man on the riverbank.
Standing in the road, I plead with him 'No!' but I'm just
a kid, so have no say. I cry all the way home, alone
on the back seat, feeling, through the many metal layers
to the boot where the creature thrashes its life away.

As for cats, they kill easily, obligate carnivores
who can't help what nature's given them. This
one's black, in profile, ears perked, the anima-
eye relaxed, observant, her fine whiskers
picked out by the light.
                              She's donned lacey
coquette-black ears, a headband, and daubed
the tip of her nose a playful black to contrast
with the white of her sclera. Bare shoulders,
kittenish, pouty lip-sticked lips, they purr.

VI

... through this composition our likeness ...

Immortalised: the girl with the dog.
All the way back to the beginning.
All the way forward to the end—even
as the earth-colours fade, the litany
of loved names:

Trixie. Jacky. Jacques. Penny. Alice.
Oscar. Tal. Lleucu. Mabon. Beca ...

I've sat in hot sand with pye-dogs,
fed and groomed them, loved them,
saved them from the shoot, wept
over those taken, been part of the pack,
brought one of them back.

Eyes and nose, shared, three dark spots
on otherwise white. Dogs are without spite—
they'll have it out, then it's done, no bitter
grudges held, no sulking ego pantomimes.

There never was an insuperable line.

VII

I love animals …

The child me played out my fantasies
with *little animals*, plastic toy cows, sheep,
horses, dogs lying down with the lions,
tigers, elephants—all safely gathered
into my own peaceable kin-dom, the toy
farm with its stables and styes, paddocks
and ponds.
          Whatever I imagined
the animals ate, it wasn't each other.
In this sanctuary, everyone belonged—
a childish vision, made of ideals,
or a soul-song singing in the blood?

Rōshi

Sometimes we may bow to cats and dogs
Shunryu Suzuki Roshi

When he was a pup, Mabon taught me
the world's ways, being Buddha-dog
in disguise, how
          what arises can and does pass away,
especially with a little help,

for Mabon was indeed in those days
a connoisseur of objects and most precise
in his choosing

for he gave lessons in non-attachment
and impermanence
          with great regularity

as on the occasion when he brought me
the wooden heart my love had given me
one anniversary,
          beautiful in its grain,
the size of my palm, symbol
of our years together.
          It
had been lifted
          for chewing
from the shelf of precious things.

The world is your path, said Mabon,
in so many words, and here's what's left
of your heart.

He gazed at me then with those puppy-brown-eyes
unclouded by thoughts of right and wrong,
all Zen in his black robe and white socks.

And so, friends, yet again, I sighed
at the world's woof ways
and bow wowed low

before raising to greater heights
the shelf of my precious things.

That Cat in Three Movements

IM Lucky

Cats leave paw prints in your heart.
                                    Anon

I The Way a Cat Interrupts

I am working at my desk: papers spread out,
books spread-eagle on certain pages, tea gone
tepid in a staining mug. Outside, the sky is about
to dissolve into saturated shades of woebegone
water colour. I have my eyes fixed not on the window,
but on the screen, where letters form into words;
I am intent on finishing. I hear the cat-flap like a shadow
somewhere in the corner of my mind. It stirs
me alert: the sudden sound of interruption
set against the syncopated time-ticking clocks.
Behind me, the soft pad of paws, then instant disruption:
up amongst my papers, sprung body blocks
the screen, outdoor footsteps leave a trail;
a pencil is teased into life, the rubber is flicked for fun.

This cat sits on the very book I'm reading from, tail
curled into a circle, feet dainty and prim. He comes
in damp from the dusk, eyes wide like an owl's.
He watches me with interest, purring rhapsodically,
flicking radar ears to and fro. Undisturbed by my scowls
and higher pitches, he seems all the more to settle methodically
into place, making this very book, this very desk,
the very space to hum out his own tune.

Once I awoke at dawn to find him vast
at my bedside, pupils like full black moons
set in a topaz sky. As I watched, he seemed
to melt into atoms, transmogrifying into air.
I turned over and went back to sleep, but the dream
held: in the morning, it echoed like a prayer.

Now I am made helpless again by this elastic shape,
this supple spine, this ecstatic whirr of insistence,
who preys upon my lap and plays at being dumb. I make
a feeble gesture, flap my hand, sigh. I could stir myself to sternness,
knock him down, lock him out, pay him off with meat or milk,
get back to work. Instead, I feel his rhythms lull my limbs long
and lower my lids. The clocks raise their volume and I sink
in between the tick and the tock to wait out his song.

II That Cat

whose fur is slid
to where your fingers spread;

whose purr splatters specifically you
(as if only you matter);

whose fish-food platter is left for manky
after The Great Show of Hunger;

who's disposed to dribble, nibble bits of digestive,
make quiver live creatures like shrews;

who eats these in the loo
on the yellow bath mat leaving them chewed up

except for, sometimes, a tail and two back legs,
a curl of innards, turned already blue;

who has a knack for snacking on the just-baked
fruit cake that's cooling on the cake-rack;

who stares you out until specifically *your* lap
no longer feels his lack;

whose orange hair sticks playfully to black;
who poops on the vegetable patch;

who is apt to back-track and leave by the cat-flap
when words shrill to: *Where's That Cat?*

III Cat's Tenth Year

For Linda and her Grey Boy

Currently, his meat must come with gravy.
Give him fish in jelly and it'll turn to flies.

He's had a phase of biting bare legs at 3am
as you sleep-walk to the loo.

The purr wakes you, then the pounce.
He draws blood, mad blooder, creature
of the night!

In spring, when wishes are for life,
he's under the blue tits' nesting box,
drooling death. He'll catch a summer rat
and eat it in half—leave the back end
with a tail, two legs and gore attached.

Autumn finds him glutting on shrews
and winter has him kill the Christmas robin
and leave it like Santa's gift in the kitchen-grotto.

Yet still—*ah, puddy tat*—
he creeps to your bed
and onto your chest
and sings you to sleep

for the warmth
and the heart to heart
pump and swish
of blood.

Two Summer Rain Songs

I

It is raining so hard,
so heavily and steadily,
that the garden birds
are missing, away among trees.

Our two hens huddle
beneath the striped recliner
that's angled and abandoned
beside the buddleia, its cushions
a sodden sheen.

The hens' tail feathers droop,
rain-beads slide along their backs
and drip from their folded wings.

The rain burbles its song—down
it comes in one long afternoon.

II

The rain, beating at the grass,
brings up earthworms. They surface
like swimmers—is that a face?
One rises against my boot,
slides along its edge,
then dives back
into the green.

Lead-up to Lockdown

March 2020

I

At the exhibition opening
a man is doing the rounds
with the same story:

I'm just back from Manchester.
Had a meal with a group
of Chinese friends.

I'm admiring the photographs
when he joins us.

Oh yes?

He seems to lean in too close,
reminding me of something—

ah yes, one of those little boys
who chases girls with a spider.

II

Teaching a day school.
At the college, I'm aware
of door handles and washing
my hands to *Calon Lân*

as Italy closes schools & universities.

III

Lunch at Llys Llewelyn—last meal out,
though we don't know it.

We talk of the new phrase:
herd immunity.

IV

We are due to teach another day school
as cases rise and still, nothing
but Johnson shaking hands
at a hospital and talk
of *taking it on the chin*.

The university acts—shifts
everything online.

V

More new terms and phrases:
Self-isolation. Lockdown.
PPE. Test, track and trace.
Social distancing. Protect
the NHS. Coronavirus.

Covid-19. Ventilators.

Friends who flew to Portugal
for a week are stuck, waiting
for a flight home, as the virus
spreads its fire and Europe
starts to close.

VI

We are told the country
is *very well-prepared.*

They let Cheltenham go ahead
& the UEFA football match
even as the WHO declare
a pandemic.

A friend's father is in a care home.
They've closed to all visitors.

One brother works in a care home
with little PPE.

When will I see him again?

VII

First death in Wales.

Schools close as parents
keep their children home.

Toilet paper's precious. A video
shows women fighting over it
in a supermarket.

Hand-sanitiser runs out.

There's talk of frontline workers,
ICU and the symptoms to check for.
Every little cough comes with a fear-note.

Meanwhile, the Spring blazes immaculate
and blossom hangs heavy on trees.

VIII

23rd March: the UK locks down at last.
We pull ourselves into our places, onto
our patches. We turn to our gardens,
social media and Zoom.

We are living through a pandemic.

Stay safe we say. *Stay safe*.

The Old Places

IM Ruth Bidgood

Looking back/at the house … It had a kind of certainty,
yet endured/tremors of hauntedness.

Ruth Bidgood

I saw Rosemary on Sunday.
We mentioned the haunted house.
In the old days, it was the ruined place
by the lake. She lives there now,
built it up from strong foundations
and made it a home again.

Of course, the crumble-down house
was made of stories told by children
who loved the thrill of walking in the dark
past the damson trees, along the paths
that twined through the thickets of blackthorn
till they came to the ramshackle ruin
in the overgrown gardens.

Back then, the house was derelict, shadowy,
its rooms open to the night's canopy.
Ferns gestured *come in* from damp corners
of abandoned rooms, but no one dared
try the stairs for fear of woodworm
and the crashing collapse of timber.
Whispers seemed to loosen memories
from the walls, emanations, tall tales
as wispy as mist, as if secrets
could be drawn from the stone
by a hand placed flat in listening mode ...

and I think of you, the old places
in your poems, the past poking through
into the present where you are
there to catch what comes,
any faint echo that makes it
through time's layerings.

It's your good habit: to inhabit
the spaces left, to lean in, an ear
to what's been, to remnants of lives
lived richly, your poet's palm pressed
against old stonework, a kind of divining
drawing out fragments like metal filings
to a magnet, readying an embrace

for the echoes you trace all the way
back to source.

Susie's Card

IM David Griffiths

It's sat on the kitchen table all week,
David's photo toasting our meals,
Meister Eckhart speaking grace.

I shared some emails with him not long
beforehand—there was that energy and bright
mindedness, even in the word-processed words.
Just days after, we heard the news, and thought
of her, the one left behind.
                      They made it together
to La Gomera to spend last times in sunshine,
wearing sun hats and shorts, going for walks,
wining and dining, laughing with friends,
fending off farewells.
                      Thank you are the words
on the front of the card, to those who sent
condolences, messages, love—and, maybe,
too, and most of all, *thank you* for his life,
for all he shared with Susie, his beloved wife.

Blue Beltane

Forget-me-nots. Their leaping fireburst.
Theirs is the blue
of multitudes,
of come-again, come-again.
They kindle borders, edges, gaps, cracks -

seeds that try for fertile ground
and find it.

They're hazing May Day, like revellers
kept too long in the dark.

Summer's Lease

For my brother, Malcolm
'How fragile we are'

Timeless pink
by the blue shed wall
rose of ages

full-headed bloom
petal on petal
of June's perfume

unfolding, as the bud
tests its hour
to open—

today's south-westerly
that soughs through the trees
freeing loose leaves

bends the rose bush
with its one perfect flower
on a tall thorny stem

scatters its petals
bouquet pink
briefest tenure

Lammas

As the year shifts there's yellow
         strip on the greenfinch wing, hypericum
by the rowan mass of starry

flowers, yolk-yellow
and
         evening primroses
         self-seeded lemony, suited
         to tissue-soft petals that sing
of here-then-gone.

All
         this in the high noon heat
of a harvesting sun.

Last of Summer

Bees among a sprawl of lavender—August
is almost spent, the sycamores tuned to the shift.

Leaves fray, tatty from what a lifetime brings;

some already litter the grass, signs
that autumn is underway, that pull

back inwards after extroversion.

We're all on loan say the leaves,
leaving.

It's been a hot summer, too much glare,
past pain pushing into the open,
fissures in the wall laid bare.

So, admit what's there, stand the stripping,
and loosen whatever has need to fall.

Autumn Equinox

For Toni

Sudden flap of crows' wings,
leaving. All month, this grit
in my shoe, bruising. Rain's
come, it's dim all day
after perpetual sun's fame.

The year hangs in balance
before its slow slide, breeze
easing the spent to loosen
their summery grip. It's
roots' time, their long thirst
quenched, and mine.

bedraggled morning
rain tapping at the bedroom
windows deepening
hawberries, last of the fuchsia,
leaves on the turn.

September's Bird

For Liz Birtles

Blackbird, *aderyn du*, you're surely used to the way
we write you into poems and songs as *messenger bird*

so don't mind me watching as, discrete amongst
the latticework branches that quiz this bright blue morning,
you hop like a thought, like a thought
                            and what have you brought me,
with your *plu du* as the leaves begin their easing off?

Sky's an open question and you're quick among the *bric-à-brac*
and there you fly, just as a single sycamore leaf flutters by
from the mother-branch of the mother-tree,
                            and as for me,
I've learned from the book I'm leafing through that Plato
was a wrestler of men, a broad-shouldered youth
famed in the Isthmian Games.
                    He's only ever been a name
till now, a mind—another bearded man,
a marble bust, almost myth.
He met Socrates and the rest, they say, is philosophy.
He never stopped wrestling, and I think of you, Liz,
and the card you sent me years ago
that lives on the board by my bed: written in 2012,
when you lived in Gwalchmai, you said:
'I was reminded of Jacob's words: *I will not
let you go, unless you bless me*'.
                    Epstein's angel upholds
the wrestling man. It takes all night, but with the dawning
comes the blessing, which is also a wounding. Tough love,
we might call it—that which is won does not come
without some kind of sacrifice.
                    And here's September, again,
the ninth month, another year, another life, three quarters done.
Aderyn du, a'i bluan sidan, the moment's messenger, among
falling leaves: take this all the way back to source.

The Dark Time

Nos Calan Gaeaf 2020

There's a full moon
behind that bank of cloud
that showed itself briefly
between the trees,
between
here and *there*, weighty, full, close.

The trees appeared to pass it
from branch to branch, with bare
brittle fingers as it rose above Llanfaelog.

It may reappear from behind Tŷ Mawr
but, for now, the cloud has taken it back
and the wind presses against the windows,
unnerving the dogs.

I return to my little lit candle, its circle
of flickering. End of the old year
in the old system, season's shift.

Down we go, then, as the dark deepens.

What shall we carry onwards?
What shall we give to the flame?

On Observing the Mulberry in November

It's true that winter
brings a certain ruination,
the way the once-perfect green
wilts, the leaves crinkling
in their drying, as the sap
withdraws

like the mulberry, last
to gain its hearts and last
to lose them—they lie
littering the ground
like little selves yielded
to the season's gravity
fallen parts of the mothertree

but the buds are already
in the flow of branch and bole
and the year's growth
adds another ring
to the heartwood.

The Start of Fox's Dissent

You saw it that day at the fair, the way word and deed
so often slide separate ways. Cousin Bradford and his friend
loosened up over that jug of beer, and though you joined them
from thirst and want of good company, one drink led to toasts
and calls for more.
                Serious, even at nineteen, you felt a kind
of treachery when they said
                    'he that would not drink should pay all'—
youthful high jinks, maybe, at a time of England's civil war,
but it grieved you sorely, them being professors of godliness
and all.
You saw the colonising move, worldish ways moving in
on you, so you scraped back your chair and laid down your groat —
'If it be so, I'll leave you'—and away you strode, out of that fair,
fellowship and family, rattled by such common trickery.

What you sought were words to follow through, the yay for yay,
the nay for nay. Our struggles and troubles with truth got to you,
but look at it this way:
                you needed that moment to set you
on your itineracy that would lead all the way to Judge Fell's door,
that stand you made in Ulverston where your words cut through
to Margaret's core so she wept for days at the truth of them,
stripped to the silent inner way.

That moment was your catalyst to go, the grit
round which the pearl would grow.

On hearing of Jo Cox's last words

June 18th 2016

My husband is out in the June sunshine
filling the bird feeder, hanging it back
by the bay tree. They have been waiting for him;
a finch is first, then a sparrow, the pair of collared doves.
Blessed are those who feed the birds,
like Saint Francis, who knew them as kin.
The roses hang, heavy with blooms,
but the fuchsia, today, its myriad scarlet droplets,
can do nothing.

She died in too much pain, that life
that served those in flight from harm,
stolen by knife and gun, her world work
done.

I watch the birds, their to and fro. Blessed
are those who build the kin-dom.

A lone feather lies in the grass,
the sunshine catching its iridescence.
A breeze is picking up, lifting it on.

Morning After

24th June 2016

In dawn light, the map showed
a wash of blue, like a dam-burst
flooding England into Wales.
Old Clwyd, inland and all along its coast,
stood water-logged, as if the river
had burst its banks again—
Glasdir homes after the deluge,
St Asaph when the Elwy rose.

Wales at sea, a land submerged.

To the greater north, a vast gold tract:
landmass holding up its solid Scottish self.
England, patched with islands of remain,
was otherwise a blur of blue

and from old Clwyd, you could stand
on stilts to gaze over the watershed
at what remained of Wales:

Gwynedd, Ceredigion, Cardiff,
Monmouthshire, Vale of Glamorgan.

Home Haibun 2021

For Meredith

9th May

As I step outside, he's perched on a branch waiting, his black feathers polished to a morning sun-sheen. I have bread and pizza scraps and he's watching with those bright keen eyes. What he will do when I throw the food is: fly down, hop sideways, alert for challengers, then peck up as much food as his big beak will hold before flying off. He's a master, rarely dropping a morsel. He often flies just a few yards into the garden, over by the greengage tree, where I see him setting down his feast to enjoy, more daintily than you'd think. Sometimes, if I've forgotten to soak the bread, he'll take it to the water bowl, dunk it till it's softened, and eat it there. We are developing a relationship. Quid pro crow.

Mum's superstition
crow flies into a window
tidings of great woe

16th May

After morning rain, the sun's come out, so I sit on the old bench outside the front door where the olive tree lives in its pot. Is it permissible to enjoy this warm sun-wash on my bare arms, while, under the same sun, Gaza is being pounded into the ground? Buildings collapse, killed children in their Eid clothes are laid in a row, one boy still with a trace of surprise on his face. A blackbird pipes its song as if to answer: *this is here, this is now*. The chestnut tree's new green translates as tenderness and its neighbour, the mulberry, is on its way back into leaf. In the distance, a collared dove soothes with its *coo coo cuk*. Life pours itself out in all its tilt and variousness, the ultimate shape-shifter. Clouds drift, blue is taken. I pick a single leaf from the olive tree and yield it to the freshening breeze.

Two male blackbirds rise
chest to chest, wings fluttering—
they chase through daisies

23 May

Our neighbour's dog barks at someone walking down the lane, while trees wave their new green in the blowy wet wind, the rowan breaking out in creamy flowerheads.

This week, I saw something new to me: two sparrows mating. The bird feeder has an arch which holds the fat ball and seed dispensers. On this arch, the female took her position, flapping her wings, tail up. The male hopped onto her back, balancing there, after which there came much mutual fluttering of wings and tail feathers. He hopped off, she fluttered—wings like eyelashes—and he hopped back on. This was repeated six times; meanwhile, other birds fed below, coming and going, oblivious.

Blossoms have set to fruit and dogs bark at people in the lane who walk, heads down, through the rain.

First cucumber crunch
fruits heavy, quick to ripen -
the birds and the bees

30 May

My life is full of birds in our garden-cum-retreat where buttercups mingle among forget-me-nots in a merry free-for-all, and daisies are cut and come again. I watch a sparrow disappear into the thick ivy that's grown up the dead trunk of a fir tree. It was snapped in two by a long-gone winter gale, but still serves as host.

Today, I experiment with a hair band and new culottes patterned with flowers, though I'm going nowhere. Here's some lipstick, robin-breast red, for May calls out colour—in me, too—ushering in summer's full-flown carnival.

The hawthorn shows me how brief its blossoms last: from Monday's creamy lace to today's sallow flowers, it's already turning to the work of growth and setting fruit. It's cast its clout and the sun's out in force, June imminent, season of extraversion. The solstice rushes towards us—so soon! The lemon tree sits in its pot outside the conservatory for the first time, enjoying (we say) the fresh air and sunshine. It is full of fruit in stages of ripening. It never stops giving. This is the summer it will feel sun direct on its leaves rather than filtered through glass. I sit beside it, like a tree feeding on light.

In a small white bowl
a lemon, one leaf attached—
I weigh the moment

6 June

In hot sunshine, a small ant whizzes around the paving stone my feet are on, a kind of scribbling that seems senseless yet likely has meaning that I am unable to translate. I lift my feet when it gets too close; I don't want it in my sandals, but I don't want to hurt it, either. I watch it pause at the edge of the shadow my feet are creating. It hesitates some moments, then, deeming things safe, moves on. I think of Blake's little fly and that summer's day; how easily some blind hand might swat any one of us out of the blue. Covid's taken a good few. I think of M and Dr T, their lives changed irradicably. Then I think of the time we found that ants had colonized our kitchen—we turned on the light and hoards skittered away to hide under the cabinets. How could this have happened? They are, it seems, highly intelligent and well-organised. Did it take one single scout to call in the masses? We had to use *stuff*—something that was slid under the fridge that lured them with sweetness. It worked quickly, but I ached for days at our treachery, and rightly— killing should hurt us. From my younger ideal of Do No Harm (a cross to nail myself to), I've learned, in a world that seems to have harm hard-wired in, to dismantle the cross. Do As Little Harm As Is Possible Under Any Given Circumstance will have to do. The ant by my feet scurries off to investigate a different paving stone and I check the ground beneath me, like a penitent Jain.

Even tinier
red clover mites zigzagging
on their way somewhere

13 June

The garden's a merry mess of colour this Sunday afternoon. We sit outside and sing to ourselves and the birds. The thrust is upwards, trees reaching to unhindered sky, maxing out their green growth.

I hear the words I'm singing—'the world is the path'. Somehow, despite the multiple challenges of embodied life, I must keep with the 10,000 things. Fidelity to all this. Some people rocket off into transcendence—up, up and away. I think of what they used to do *for God:* austerity, self-flagellation, multifold punitive treatments of the flesh. Those who rejected the world and mortified themselves in preparation for being eternally Up—does such lived unkindness *really* maketh a saint? Humans have a history of experiment, but that one seems a loveless wrong turn. The world is the path—where else? The visible *and* the invisible, ascended *and* descended ... Too much heaven can blind as much as any deep plunge into materialism's dark literalisms.

As we go in to make some tea, I glance at the blue Celtic cross on our wall in the conservatory. Did the more insightful ancient ones circle that centre point where polarities meet because they understood *y lle rhwng*? If the cross is a body, the gathered locus is the heart. How to live from this centre is my ponderance.

Chestnut tree fullness
on its way to prophethood—
sky filtered through leaf

4 July

Cock pheasant's beneath the bird feeder again, his wattles the colour of fuchsia flowers, his plumage burnished by the Sunday sun. The littler birds are scattering seeds as they rummage through them for favourites and he, below, pecks them up, a perfect symbiosis. He is often here, alone or with his two hens. Then, he's like a comic king with his ladies-of-the-court. They'll suddenly appear, an entourage, round the corner by the bay tree, in single file, with the king leading in regal procession. Now, it's just him and his pennies from heaven. I try to watch tactfully, through the window, so as not to disturb him, but he eventually notices a small movement of my hand. His head goes up and he gazes at me as I gaze at him. I feel as if he is assessing me for danger. I am gratified when he drops his head and continues his seed-work. I back away gently and leave him to it. When I next look, he's gone.

Pheasant pecks among
the oregano, sunshined
to a high-gloss sheen

From *Lost Sequence with John*

For John Wright

I

I walk among the ash trees after a day's rain,
checking branches for die-back, tell-tale signs of rot.
Nothing but autumn here, drawing the leaves down:
mulch for the roots—the strange way life
feeds on itself.
          My palms stroke down bark
seeking a prayer to spare these trees
as afternoon's milky light deepens into first night.

II

I want to tell you about the rain, how all day
it's lent a shine to dull surfaces. This morning,
I pulled the blind: green-brown dripping
against grey.
          A deep crack in the white wall
lengthened, curled—slug, its horns forward,
on its way somewhere.
          Later, I walked with the rain
pittering against my hood. All along the path,
the dog caught and carried the ball,
in it wholly for the game.

III

I thought of her this morning, Alice,
as I passed the graves, the names
hidden now by May's upward trend.

In amongst the mess of grass
and forget-me-nots, the Buddha
was touching the earth for witness.

Mental Fly

A fly buzzes against glass,
taps hard, scribbles and dots
up and down the window.

It can see all that blue beyond, is called
by it to fly. But there's this block it knocks
itself against, over and overall that bombination,
the energy spent working the same old pane.

Such a shame when, with a sideways shift,
the wide open door offers exit.

Ambulant

All month, the clement blue of it
dependable (though death came)
pristine bumper green, the year
coming to its head.
                  Today, a shift—
rain finally in the forecast, the air utterly still
as if waiting for that first tear.

The grasses spill their seed onto my bare arms
as I pass, as if my pores might be the fertile soils
they seek and Lleucu's sleek coat is a seed bed
for fescue, clover, meadowsweet -

seed begetting seed, doing what it does, passing
itself on, the quick of it, before the year turns
beyond what it can do and the husk is caught
by that colder wind and blown off into the big blue.

Veg Patch

In response to Meredith Andrea's 'Phacelia Tanacetifolia'

Everything furthers, they say, so
what's the learning of the veg patch?
Each spring, for years, he's diligently
cleared beds and planted beans, carrots,
peas in rows, weeded with new
sun on his back

        this time will be different

but by June, the growthbursting everything
has outrun his time, crowded out the crops
with what we call weeds   their outlandish zeal
their wild push and thrust, their spillage everywhere

and you can see it in him, the defeat, the overwhelm,
grieving wasted energies, the time it all needs
that he hasn't got, the day to day care
to save young plants from that
which will engulf them.

So, here it is, abandoned—a triumph
of ferns, brambles, umpteen grasses,
nettles, cleavers, docks

even a dog-rose, lolling in the corner,
has settled in along the fence
and is pushing its suckers
in among the beds

and I think of what you grew
to make the clay workable

tansies to dream the summer through
a smoke of flowers for the bees

and here is something a poem brings
steps for a year, one more clearing

then packets of seed to cover the patch
with a long summer-blue insectary

till the time-rich time comes
when the gardener in him

can be present again.

The Teaching of Trees

IM Lleucu (2002-2016)

The sycamores that line the boundary
between us and the Carreg Wen field
look worse for wear in this wind that tugs
at what remains of their tatty leaves.
Through their boughs, glossed with ivy,
sky shifts its colours—slate to milk to blue—
and I think of the way age dries us,
turns and twists our edges, pulls us
to yield our fine summer stuff.

Out front, the great chestnut tree
we planted from small is dropping
its first crop, its fruit in spiky burrs.
We find them among the spent leaves,
the split outer casing, the shiny gloss of nut.

We buried the sweet white and chestnut of her,
fourteen summers long (oh precious seed),
beneath the red maple, and the ground
took her to itself like a nurse saying *there, there*

and what can we do but bend in the wind
like trees obedient to what seasons bring
love lending its creatures to each other
in its inscrutable fructifying way.

Aberffraw

Ynys Môn, Wales
53° 11' 0" North, 4° 27' 0" West

This is where we came when Oscar died, when I'd lost my voice
missing him. It's where we've walked all our dogs, along the estuary's
edge, as Afon Ffraw ebbs and flows like the fortunes of the village.

It's here there was once a port where fishing ships moored
and Matholwch's mythships, too, when he sailed, King of Ireland,
flying his bright silks, to seek union with the Isle of the Mighty,
coming to feast in Aberffraw and lie that night with Branwen.

It's where the great storm of 1331 upheaved the beach, sand
silting up the harbour's depth, forming the dunes we walk among,
now steadied by grasses.
              When southwesterlies blow in off the Irish sea,
any little boat with a mast whines and tickers eerily, and sand skims
fast over itself, blowing up off Traeth Mawr, where waves crash

and would have crashed back when the royal court was here,
when Llys Llywelyn wasn't a nice little café, but capital
of the Kingdom of Gwynedd.
              Once, after a storm, when the river flooded
big over the bridge, it left a small blue boat smashed by the wall
with a mess of seaweed and rubbish strewn over the road.
              High tides and winds can still
bring trouble in, but who'd think it on a sunny day like this,
even as the sands shift underfoot.
It's August and hard to park, the beach bustling with visitors,
and dogs splashing across the river, chasing chucked balls, v
oices and barks bouncing off the village walls—
              but when you're out some late afternoon,
and a winter gale's tearing up the Ffraw,
you can almost hear Matholwch's horses
screaming over the dunes.

Sŵn cŵn
          dros y cae
yn yr haf gwyrdd
a phedair gŵydd
          yn hedfan
tua'r machlud

Da ni'n dal i gasglu golau
a blodau gwylltion

a sŵn cŵn   cyn y nos
yn galw ni adra

Dogs bark
                across the field
in summer's green

as four geese fly
towards sunset.

We are still
gathering light
& wild flowers

as dogs, just before nightfall,
call us home.

Noson Hydref

Mae'n nos nawr. Noson fawr.
Jyst ti a fi a'r distawrwydd.

Gwynt tywyll tu allan, glaw ar y ffenest:
patrymau gonest fel alawon cyfarwydd.

Autumn Evening

It's night-time, now. Wrapping night.
Just you and me and the silence.

Dark wind outside, rain at the window:
honest patterns like familiar tunes.

Crab-Apple Sequence

Ein Hoff Le garden, Thursday 25th June 2020

After Wallace Stevens

I

I tell the dogs
we will go out
'in a minute'.

Their ears droop
at the phrase.

II

Hottest day of the year.

My hair is in bunches
that stick out sideways.

'You look twelve.'

When I was twelve
I'd cut off my hair
to look like my brothers.

III

The dogs are joyous,
ears as up as up, when
'in a minute' arrives.

IV

On the swing-seat
deep in the garden.

A butterfly flutters past.

The pond is full of bulrushes.

V

I swing in the bare breeze, the sun
like a master smelter.

Whatever is invisible in us,
particulars are where love lives.

VI

In between thinking aloud on the page,
I pitch the ball.

Dogs: a self-filling well of play.

VII

In this heat, I leave
                              space
between throws.

The dogs pant, alert, in the shade,
while the mock-orange flowers
waft a perfumed munificence.

VIII

The little crab-apple tree,
laden with fruit, lives in hope
of dissemination.

Where does 'hope' start and end?

Nature's 'wastefulness'
might be called
'generosity'.

IX

I'm wearing a straw hat, too,
which reminds me of something -
ah, yes, *Beverly Hillbillies*.

Can we ever empty fully
from the past?

There's the clear empty space
sages speak of which are moments
when we're burned back to whatever
consciousness is

and then there's the everyday
reservoir of being here
and of *having lived*.

X

I wore dungarees in the 70s.
Now they're back. Life—
its circles and spirals.

This big sheer sky
opens and opens.

Love the questions, and live them,
Rilke said.

XI

My ex-student, H, is in her summer,
good green leafage in her
oakly branchings.

We now sign our messages: xx

III Saint John's Wort

The hypericum bush is covered in waxy yellow stars, the flowers that are said to bloom around John the Baptist's birthday, the 24th June. This year, they're a little late, but what's a couple of weeks in the life of a summer? Our garden is full of memories: trees or shrubs carrying something of the person who gifted them. Olive, rowan, mahonia, sweet chestnut—so many interconnections. I think of who gave us the St John's Wort, so many years ago, when she was still speaking to us. The flowers carry a story of healing, but not everyone knows how to soften what's stony within them. People lose their heads—and John did, literally, though he was healer, baptiser, prophet. Life's vagaries. I don't hold anything against this beautiful shrub, so well grown and healthy, thriving in its place by the rowan tree. It was a small bush when given, and now look at it.

Paracelsus knew
even in those early times—
flowerherb heartlift

Ting

For Meredith Andrea

Fire depends on wood for flame
and here's the return, right with this patch of mottled grass
this morning its patches picked out
                                            and each wet lit blade
shows as individual for a micro-moment
though the lot of grass is to be plain,
plural, underfoot

like us, seen from space—microbial—
all that we are, all *all* of it
unparticularised   mass elements, except
for where there's a kind of regard

so what to say about spring this year
when you feel its push like a birthing?

The birds are at the nesting boxes and I'm tired of rules
ready to let go my dead-headedness

like dad's hydrangeas, their brown and brittle flowerheads
overwintered, sheltering the buds, serving the new
but now they need to go

and the *i ching* gave me *ting*, the cauldron: remove
stagnating stuff and use the pot to boil off dross

to do that (it says) you must let go the wood of you
feed it to the flame.

Key

Every morning before work, John Cage watered his house plants.
Of course, there is music, even in this, and it's wise to start
each day with an act of care, listening into leaves, tending roots.

This morning, I water the begonia, the orchid and maranta.
I've let them go dry. The rubber tree, the dracaena, the Xmas
cacti. And look at the dust dimming the Buddha, along the shelf

where the photos are—the dead ones smiling out of their frames.
Do the little things. Wipe away dust. It's an act of tuning,

Abel's Angel

Olive wood, for a start, from Bethlehem.
Angel of music and word, bought
from Abel one Xmas.
                              I may have meant
to give it away, but it so fitted my hand.
Its grainy sheen & little violin
paused me so that now,
these years later, we are
each other's

for, after all, true angels
are never flimflam.

They say *stop* & *listen*
for the news you need.

This one is on the side of bending
an ear and, as it's solstice, where we are
deepest in dark, I lean myself in, to hear.

Deer Heart

Creature of forest, eye-lashed, big eared
from listening—let her come to you
in her own time, like moments come
sometimes, unbidden, to stop you in the kitchen
with a little revelation: *this too is how it can be.*

Sit waiting, then, your back against a tree,
at the edge of her green. Perhaps she will come
to your deep-hearted calling, but only when she trusts
your stillness and always on her own terms.

Rowing

For my brothers

We're in the middle of the lake
when our number's called.

I am rowing, not very well.
I am the eldest and biggest.

I have blisters forming by my thumbs.
Somehow, the boat keeps spinning.

My father shouts instructions from land,
which makes me splash water into the boat.

A crowd gathers to watch.
Left oar! Now right!

The boat makes spectacular circles.
My brothers fall silent.

My father's words fly upon the waters:
Both oars together! *Bloody hell*!

I get the boat close enough—
they reach us with a hook.

The crowd parts as we get off.
Nobody claps.

How You Won Her

It was your voice she fell for. You sounded
like a gentleman. And when you called
that New Year's afternoon, after her shift,

she was in her slip on the sofa, her work skirt
slung over the back of the arm-chair.
You saw it, as you hovered in the doorway,

let in by Patsy, and excused yourself a moment
—something about the car. You gave her time
to leap from under her rug, her mother bustling

to put the kettle on and *tidy yourself, hinny.*
All afternoon by the fire, you sat with the women
drinking tea, eating scones and barm cake,

till she loved you and would say yes.

Pugilist 1

So they take you to the far end of the playground that first break. Lads crowd, kicking at your brogues that look too new, mark you out, but what can you do when your father's bought them for a bob or two, spit and polished them to a sheen you can see your face in, showed you how to lace them tight, straightened your cap, straightened his back—and your mother's waved you off down the lane, hard-boiled egg in your satchel and *this is a new start, doesn't our boy look smart?*

When you look back, they're still there, your mother's square of hanky a speck of white in thin morning air.

The jacket's too big, you get there hot. You give yourself away first thing when you say *Oy'm Bob*. Brum boy in a little Bath school. The sniggers from the desks behind make you hate the way your face flames.

All the week, you're picked on by the boys, heckled when you speak. You fetch up home with your new brogues scuffed, your jacket pockets torn. Your nose has bled into your tie so you cop it from your mum. You cry all night long.

Then you tell them what's been going on.

She says it's just a settling in, like chickens in a coop. Turn the other cheek, rise above the throng.

Your father, though, he says, *No, it's wrong*. He takes you down the shed, shows you moves to use with your feet and fists. Never mind what she says. You've got to fight your way round. You've got to *fight* them, yes? This is the start of becoming a man.

All week after, in the corner of the schoolyard, out of sight of the masters and their canes, you give what you get, and more, with fists and feet, till the other sore and black-eyed lads meet you one morning at the gate with sheepish grins

and let you in.

Pugilist 2

You've snuck away to the county fair, leaving the stale air of the
house with its rows and silences, the stink of your mother's
stew. Your father's bending, now, at the waist from the shrapnel
in his back from the Great War, and you've double-trenched the
carrot patch after school to save him the pain.

Now, the lass you like is smiling by the circus tent, but you've
heard the crowd, seen the ring and the two gloved boxers
parading in, and you're pulled that way to roar for the scrawny
feather-weight who, after going two long rounds, with a sharp
neat hook, lands one hard on the nut of the other bigger bugger
such that he staggers, lurches, rolls his eyes backwards and
finally falls. Eight, nine, ten … and the victory, it's yours.

Lament

The father, now no more a father, cries,
Ho Icarus! where are you?

                           Ovid

How you fell
           how—
and why were we so high
for you to fall so far?

Your slip was almost a jump and then
down you went down
pin-head small and o my son
                       until
a splash
        a tiny of white
            was you
               landed.
                   My scream
was one of those that stop in the throat:
an audible shock-awful head full of hush.

You were gone from me, then.

Years I've spent, recreating you. Reaching
for our last fingers-outstretched, tips-to-tips.

Rosebuds in Blue

I enter the room of mirrors and take from the hanger
my mother's dress—the bluebell-blue ball gown,
the one she wears in that tinted photo when dancing
waltz on the patio and kissing my father like a film star.

You can see air under her Cinderella slippers
and flirt in her glance.

I wear my mother's sky, her oceans, in that dress.
I twirl before the many mirrors of the mirrored room
floating in blue gauze stitched with rosebuds
into a moment that dances away and away.

Too Lonely

It was too lonely for her in that house of shadows.

Lonely she whispered to the walls and windows.
Lonely she cried to the corridors.

And she'd seek in all the cobwebbed corners.
And she'd seek among the high wooden rafters.
And she'd lean her ear against the beams, the jousts,
that creaked like a galleon all night long
as she listened, lost in that timbrous house.

She'd try out every dusty room, brushing filaments
from her hair and she'd push against shutters locked
against forever.
                In the night she'd dream
her long-banished song, turning on her side to feel
for the glass beside her.

'For I can snore like a bullhorn, sleep like a sluggard
in the dark rugged caveling by the curling, far-flung sea ...'

And she'd wake aching with the first light,
heat at her temples, salt on her lips and *lonely*
whispering is the corners of her room.

Soul's Bird

That bird you found
on the side of the road—
you brought it home,
put it in the rabbit hutch,
and fed it each day while
its wing mended.

Now it's ready, you weep
for the way things always leave—

but

when this bird finds its flight
when this bird after your tending
flies first onto the branch
then the roof then up
into the sky and away

and your heart floods
with its myriad wishes,

that is the time
to lift your hand
and raise your voice

to call after it
not
      'come back,
stay with me for ever'

but
      'yes!
                  fly!

For what am I
      but a bird?

Wish me the same!'

Aunty Toss Comes for a Visit

Aunty Toss is in the kitchen
with Dad, giving him hell
over a frying pan he isn't
doing something right with.
Where Mum is God only knows;
maybe it's too early for her, maybe
she's keeping well out of it.

(Aunty Toss found her brandy
the other day, tucked away
at the back of the cupboard,
and gave her a sermon
on the ills of drink.)

Now, Dad stands by the sink
like the little lost brother
his sister still thinks he is.
Never mind *engineer*.
Never mind *man of the world*.

Glancing up, he sees me—
his little girl, his eight year old—
hesitant in the doorway

as Aunty Toss flaps at him
with her long thin hands.

At a Victorian Victualler's c.1890

After Edouard Manet's Bar at the Folies-Bergère

For Jill Teague

She has the look of being there—*A drink, Sir?*—
and, equally, elsewhere, because
how else otherwise could she stand it,

knowing that when she bends to reach
for the brandy bottle from the lowest shelf,
the best brandy the whiskered gentleman
has ordered—*a goodly glass, ma dear, to stir the blood*—

she'll feel his eyes comb through her hair, right to the scalp,
loiter at that narrowest point of her girdled waist,
then hunger like hot hands at her buttocks
hid amongst all that frock

so that when she turns, in that half moment, she'll catch
him at it, his shifty gaze shifting upward, a wet mouth
at her bosom, briefly, briefly, because he's a *gentleman,*
before settling back on her face.

She'll smile, politely, pretend not to notice
as she glugs the liquor into the snifter, places it
on the coaster, lets his fingers fold over hers
a moment (the damp heat of his touch).

Still, she'll wonder, as she leans towards him
on strong wrists she scented earlier with lilac mist,
how it might be to be his mistress. He's brought her
two pretty blooms for being his *best girl*. That's them
in the fluted glass right there on the bar.

How easy such men are.

First Mother

she is long-lonely in the dank cave
her belly full of almost-child
has two damp sticks won't make a flame
cold is the same is the numbing same

he's been gone three light-ups now
in the outside stuff that falls and wets

her hunger frets her fingers itch
she feels her way to cold cave's edge
to squat and wait chewing on chaff

then the sungod gold breaks through
when cloud-mess splits grassland lit
greens her eyes fix on figure distant
her belly kicks she smooths the round
strains her eyes to see him come

I'll Give You *Chick*

So there was this woman who climbed the gate
and strode among them brandishing the broom
she'd been sweeping the yard with;

this eight-stone woman, her hair spilling from its comb,
keys jangling from her belt, pinny floured from bread-baking
like some well-fashioned mother.

Well, she scattered them like naughty boys for their bother,
calling them each by their real names.

They tried to duck and whoop, wolf-whistle,
blow raspberries and call at her lewdly,
all the old tricks but

she knew their paltry games and was after them
like a wilded mother hen.

She blew those puffed-up roosters into a spin
their heads colliding

and saw them off in a flurry of squawks,
white feathers flying.

Going to Hell

One woman makes a din, two women a lot of trouble,
three an annual market, four a quarrel, five an army,
and against six the Devil himself has no weapon.

The magazine lies open on the glass table
and though I want a sunlit peaceful sit—
time out, a chance to look away for a while—
I can't abandon the *sow at the gates*
of the slaughterhouse, the close up shot,
the doomed intelligent eye, pink skin,
freckles, blonde hair, birth mark

and now I've looked, I can't unsee, unfeel
the tsunami-sweep of body-woe
answering body-woe

and who *then* should show up, charging
over the hill, but Dull Gret in her apron
and armour, pots and pans clanking
in her basket. This time she means it.
She's headed for the mouth of hell
with her voice raised in a rallying yell
and I'm at her side, making hullabaloo,
oh yes, and others join, warriors all, fierce

to melt that whole fiasco all the way down
to the frozenmost embers of treachery.

Selfies for Peace

*Response to Wanda Garner's film 'Real Women of the World',
written during Putin's invasion of Ukraine, March 2022*

For Eileen

They carried her over rubble on a stretcher,
her belly huge with imminent child,
the bombed-out maternity hospital

behind her in splinters, dazed women,
children, doctors, nurses staggering
out of its smoking shell.

Now, as I watch each woman's face in the film
slide past, standing for peace, for solidarity,
each selfie a small act of resistance, an appeal

against what is here again, another man's war,
your face appears, friend over decades, closely
interwoven into my own life's fabric

and I picture us, two women of Wales, as them,
on a crowded platform somewhere: I'm pushing
through the throng, everyone desperate, everyone

pushing, when I glimpse you, in your dog-walking fleece,
your blonde bob, created in peacetime, awry. Shouting
across the many heads your name, your name, I start

swimming, it feels, against an impossible current
as the one train blows its whistle to leave.

In this story, the woman safely births her baby
and you hear me over the hubbub, turn, our eyes
meet, arms stretch, hands reach, grasp, hold on

past happy endings or make-do starts to where
we're all part of what is or may be, each life
a legacy of hope, of *keep trying*, of *never give up*

on the pregnant potentials for peace.

Nana's Cabinet

Remembrance Day November 2020

The gale has shaken
the last apples
from the tree.

They litter the grass
yellows, greens and reds
this blue breezy morning

the fallen that were ready
to drop, being ripe.

She kept a shrine for him
on her glass cabinet,
the son who fell

his framed photo central, young man
whose clock stopped at twenty three.
The uncle I never met, he is
forever uniformed, surrounded
by poppies and crosses
to never forget

Cecil who went to war
dapper and kind, and never
came home

burned alive in a bombed-out tank
in Libya's desert.

When the front door knock came
to the house on Emily Street, it was Rita
who answered, absent-mindedly,
eldest sister, full of child.

The telegram boy stood on the step
angel of death she saw his face
saying it all—in the living room
they read out the words
we regret to announce that Trooper Cecil Hulme
has been killed in action in Tobruk.

His mother fell to the floor,
his sister's womb fell
the child fell,
the family
the father
who felt his tears
seep through his fingers, the shock
killing him softly.

Just another Tommy cut down
Desert Rat in the sand holding the line
against Rommel's tanks fighting
to the last man and the last round.

If Only

She knew, if the call came, he'd enlist.
If things got worse, as the papers forecast,
he'd be one of the first to go. Hero. That's
what he was, her good boy.
                              He'd played
the boyhood games of kill or be killed,
first with sticks, then with the toy guns
his dad had sanctioned, the village lads
splitting into sides, forming ranks.

It's just a phase. Boys will be boys.

As the talks failed, and failed some more,
and another war became more and more the word
on every street corner, she felt her stomach pitch
towards panic. All those years of love and care
for this? He was young still, but old enough.

At dinner, she ladled soup from the pan
lost in a secret plan to slip to his bedside
as a deep-night shadow, his father's hammer
in her hand. It would only take a well-aimed blow
to break his trigger finger for good, maybe two
or three more for good measure, just enough
to keep him home.
                              And wouldn't she bear
his screams, his shock, his hate? He'd understand in time
her good intentions. She'd tell him it was to save him,
a tough-love deed born from a mother's love

but when she waved him off, her proud soldier boy,
and the telegram came two years later that sank her
to the floor *we regret to inform you ... killed in action ...*

she wept for weeks behind closed doors, and wished.
She wished. She wished. How she wished.

Ready, Lads?

Just before he blew the whistle
he felt a hot, clear rage.

It flooded him, and his eyes
were surely bloodshot, for all
he could see was red.
                              The men
around him—lads, boys, pals, chums—
glowed in a red mist, and he loved them,
more than ever, these brave, disposable
nuts and bolts in the killing machine.

But it was rage that made him ready.
He knew that over that top, they would
each find the bullet that would send
them home.

            'Ready, lads?'

Into the arms of the enemy, at that stricken
mud-thick front, they ran, stumbled, fell.

Moment

The thing I'm grateful for, Dad, is that I was there.

I'd lingered—I don't know why—but, leaving,
I didn't leave.
On the threshold of the ward,
I called: *love you*.

Love you too. (Last thing you said.)

         One moment
and I'd have followed the others
to the lift.
      But, beginning to turn, I turned back
to see you blur, as some wild wave swept
through you.

The plastic cup you'd reached for clattered
to the floor, and I saw you'd wet yourself.

Back by your side, calling to the nurses
for help, I found you already gone
from your eyes.

You never came back from where the stroke
took you, though we sat at your side for two weeks
taking turns in a bedside vigil of hope

until it became simply waiting
          and on the Monday night
you passed, I was there, my hand in yours
as you breathed your last breath of air.

Anniversary of Dad's Death

22nd November

I've been busy all day but at last
I sit down to talk to you. Can this poem
be a table where we pull up chairs
and catch up with each other? I've made it
for that purpose. Look: it has a clean white cloth
spread out, onto which we place our words
like tea cups, saucers, plates. I was going
to say *fancy cakes* but you interrupt: *make mine
a piece of cheddar with a hunk of bread.
And I'd rather a beer than tea.*

Of course. Hello Dad.

Death. It's a funny thing. Sometimes
it's a blessing. Bodies are made to go
off into the smoky blue yonder, like yours did
ashes to ashes or down into earth, *dust
to dust* and that does seem to be that
and yet—
               I knew
you had to go. When younger, I'd watch
your vigour and wonder: how would you ever
stop? But when your hair whitened and your back
began to bend, I glimpsed your ending.

Little Pooh you say now (your pet name for me, your voice)
and tender crumbs gather on the table top.

Is it treacherous, years on, to say that it had to come?
The ether is thick with the terror of those who die appallingly.
Some deaths, though, are more like leaves falling from autumn trees.

You drain your glass. Then it's time. Well, Dad, wherever you are,
it's been good talking.

Same time next year?

Viriditas

The questions come,
opening a silence.

I reveal empty hands
that say, *Look, nothing*—

but a chill breeze
tumbles a dead leaf
over the paving stones

and it's my ear that turns me
in its direction before I see it.

Crisp sycamore, what's left
of a year, a life's, cycle

and as my ear tunes me
I feel the sound of that
small bit of—can I call it *kin?*—
so distant and done-with

and yet

life's laws are inscrutable
the leaf going where winter
takes us

though green seems
to keep coming

so in this leaf go I, blown
by that breathy *spiritus*

the leaf yielding like Hildegard's feather
carried on the breath she sang to, tuned to,
O *circulus toti, that can neither be understood,
nor divided, nor begun nor ended* ...

The dead leaf, in singing its small parable
in my company, opens me again to my question:

if everything speaks, who am I
not to listen?

Threshold

December 2018

IM Jay Ramsay

Walk with the dogs
in the last days of December,
the whole year lying as shadow behind us
in this late-afternoon
winter sunshine.

*The gone is gone is
to be learned from ...*

It's midge-mild,
my fleece too warm.
The dogs pant
as they gallivant
after the ball, down and round
the seven acre field.

On return, note the way
the low sun gilds the tree tops.

Note Dad's Monbretias
up already, their green fire lick
at the base of the cherry tree.

Note the clutches of snowdrops
those little ambassadors
of *come again*.

Jay wrote in my copy of his *Dangerous Book:*

*through the long winter nights
and always in hope of Spring.*

Ah, friend, that was on the 5th.
You made it almost to the end
of the month, the year.

Spring's emblems are everywhere,
even as the last day comes.

On return, note the budding, even
among Winter's remains. Note
the belly kick, Montbretia flame.

Ready to start the whole thing again?

Friar Francis

Oremus pro Invicem

He carries it in his eyes
the trickle of tributary swelled
to deep river that's wended
through thicket and briar,
disappeared long years deep
underground, only to bubble
out into open pasture at last.

His face shows he knows the way
life's hardnesses can and do
knock bits off us all, spoil
the ideas we are in thrall to,
ideals of perfection, those palaces
of glass we start off with
that have to shatter to let
us out into the flow.

Same goes for trajectories
we thought were ours. 'Live the life
that's yours' goes the chorus
'not the one you thought was yours'—

so learn softness in the face of stone hearts,
pliability in the face of stone minds,
flow in the face of *set*

loving the creaturely *as thy self*
is the best bet, calling them brother, sister,
father, mother—even the sun, even the moon,

even this patch of earth
called *you*.

Thank You, Heart

Out into the place of birds, to be permeated by their surround-sound piping & peeping. Long afternoon November shadows lie upon the grass, as the sun, after rain, slips towards the west, bright among the yellowing mulberry leaves. The sweet chestnut rustles in the bare breeze, more a breathing, & here are the nearer sounds of each leaf dropping, the crisp edge meeting the ever-ready ground. Back the way of windfalls, hollowed-out by crows and blackbirds, &, by the steps, snapdragons are still in what must be their final flush of flower.

There's no saying how the year will end, the month, the week, the hour. This is our inheritance, to abide with such unknowables—yet constants shape us, too, so thank you, heart, for your ever-faithful undercover work, & another night follows its day.

Sun bows out, stage right,
coral curtain-call flourish
as moon rises left

Notes on the poems

Opening epigraph

From Seán Street's poem 'Spring in the Suburbs' (*Journey into Space*, 2022, Shoestring Press).

Anima/l

This set of poems are ekphrastic responses to some photographs by Hungarian art-photographer Flóra Borsi from her *Animeyed* collection which can be viewed here: https://floraborsi.com/animeyed-self-portraits

'Insuperable line' refers to the famous argument on sentience put forward by eighteenth-century philosopher Jeremy Bentham, in *The Principles of Morals and Legislation* (1789), where he argued that there is no insuperable line between species, the question being not 'Can they *reason?* nor Can they *talk?* but, Can they *suffer?*'

I used quotations by Borsi to preface each poem, from a short piece posted on the online community site *Bored Panda.*

The Dark Time

Nos Calan Gaeaf is the Eve of the first day of winter, November 1st (Halloween).

The Start of Fox's Dissent

Quotations are from *The Journal of George Fox* [1694]. Margaret Fell of Swarthmoor Hall, Ulverston, married George Fox after her husband, Judge Fell, died. She became known as 'the mother of Quakerism'.

The Morning After

The map referred to is the one that appeared on the BBC EU referendum results website.

Aberffraw

Matholwch and Branwen are characters in the Second Branch of the *Mabinogion*.

Going to Hell

The epigraph is a Dutch proverb.

Selfies for Peace

This poem was part of the 'Grandmothers' Peace Creative Group' on exhibition at Plas Bodfa, Anglesey/Ynys Môn. Wander's Garner's film can be viewed on YouTube.

Ready Lads?

The poem was inspired by Ernst Junger *(Diary,* 1918), in which he talks about the boiling and incomprehensible rage that seized the men on the battlefield.

Friar Francis

This poem was written while keeping company with our patio stone figure of Saint Francis. *Oremus pro Invicem* means 'Let us pray for each other'.

Milton Keynes UK
Ingram Content Group UK Ltd.
UKHW031823250824
447283UK00003B/48